The Analyst Mindset

Data Driven Decisions

By Hugo Soto

I want to dedicate this book to my two most trusted business advisors.

My mother & My wife

Thank you

Special Thanks to Collectiv.

For believing in my words and ideas enough to help me take this book across from a rough draft to a finished book.

Collectiv are Microsoft data platform and Power BI experts who empower C-Suite executives by radically improving data analytics, planning, and AI processes across the enterprise. With passion and experience, Collectiv delivers world-class measurable outcomes via strategy, consulting, advising, and programs. Empower your enterprise with Collectiv.

www.goCollectiv.com

CONTENTS

Foreword

Part 1: Bird's Eye View

Introduction

The Human Factor

Data-Oriented Mindset

  The Importance of Curiosity

  The Scientific Method

  Knowledge Needed

Analyst Project Lifecycle

  Define Work

  Acquire Data

  Transform Data

  Present Information

  Moving Forward

Part 2: In the Trenches

Narrowing the Scope

Data Mining

  Always start with what you have

  Explore adjacent resources

Data Cleaning

Standardize
  Categorize
  Focus on what you need
  Working across systems
 Targeted Data-Finding
  Reason backwards
  Connect to the bigger picture
  Cutting up the questions
 Calculated and Derived Data
  Understanding assumptions
  Start with universal calculations
  Custom calculations
  Assumptions and risks of custom calculations
 Deep Dive
  Finding outliers
  Data hierarchies
  Root cause analysis
  Five Whys
  Fishbone diagram
  The scientific method
 Reporting
  Know your audience
  Know your data
  Double-check your work
  Emphasize the importance and impact
  Paint a story

- Visualizations
  - Consistency principle
  - Time horizon
  - Data and charts
    - Pie Charts
    - Line graphs
    - Geo maps
    - Bar Graphs
    - Summary cards
    - Scatter plots
- KPI
- Dashboards
  - Purpose
  - Method
    - Graphics
    - Charts
  - Aesthetics
    - Tell a story with your dashboard
  - Color
  - Maintaining the dashboards
- Closing Remarks

FOREWORD

There is no shortage of bright minds, there is no shortage of resources, and there is no shortage of opportunities in this world. All that stands between today and a bright future for you, your company, or your country, are the decisions that you make every day.

We have dedicated our lives and our business to helping people with those decisions. Whether it is a financial, real estate, logistics, or construction company. Whether you have a team of two, or a team of a thousand. It is crucial now, more than ever, to make strong strategic decisions using all the tools we have at our disposal.

We believe that this book, can help people across the world, because we have seen first-hand what good information, and good decision making can do for a company and the lives of its employees.

We hope you enjoy this book as much as we did, and it helps your decisions moving forward.

The team at Collectiv

PART 1: BIRD'S EYE VIEW

INTRODUCTION

Since the invention of writing, humans have been keeping track of things. From crop records in papyrus scrolls to profit and loss statements in today's corporations.

As the data recorded becomes bigger and more complex, it gets more and more difficult to interpret accurately. Today, business leaders everywhere hire entire teams of highly specialized people to extract, analyze, and summarize big sets of data. From this data, they extract useful and actionable intelligence by which to make their day-to-day decisions. This practice has given business leaders everywhere unprecedented visibility. This enables them to act quickly and effectively in accordance with changing market needs.

With today's growing technology, more and more data-collecting tools are available to growing corporations. Also, more market data is now available for purchase. The only challenge is finding people with the correct skills to make heads or tails of all the available information.

According to the Bureau of Labor Statistics, employment of computer and information research scientists, including data analysts, is projected to grow by 27 percent from 2016 to 2026. Median pay is set to be $81,390 per year.

I am writing this book to help people build the necessary mindset, and skill set to address this shortage in the market. I have spent many years taking data and turning it into actionable intelligence for all sorts of projects and corporations and I hope that my experience with all these projects can help those who are entering the field.

Whether you're a small business owner or a student hoping to get a job as a data analyst, this book will guide you through the common-sense practices that are usually only learned through extensive experience in the field. Even though I have a lot of technical expertise, I'm making a conscious decision not to make this a technical book. Here's why:

First, technology changes rapidly. By the time this book is published, new versions of the current software will be available and data analysis tools will have changed. There will also be new players in the market offering innovative ways to slice and dice the data. I believe the best sources for technical information will always be the publishers of whatever software you decide to use. This is why I always recommend getting the truth on it straight from the source.

The second reason is that every analyst is different. Everyone thinks differently. Everyone understands and processes information differently. Thus, creating a technical book on the subject would only end up being useful for the small percentage of the population whose mind works like mine.

By switching the perspective of this book from a technical piece of literature to a conceptual piece, I hope to create work that is useful to any new analyst attempting to make sense of their new role, or any business (or process) owner trying to start using data to make better business decisions.

This book will not be very helpful to you if:

- You're already an advanced data analyst looking to sharpen your craft
- You're expecting technical advice on any data analysis software

THE HUMAN FACTOR

There is one truth that applies to all data which we can use as an axiom to understand the role of an analyst. All data has a human factor to it. Whether it is an individual sitting with a pencil recording his observations or a high-level executive deciding on what he wants recorded or tracked from his business processes. Understanding the human factor contained in the data can be the difference between good data analysis and half-baked information that can lead to bad decision-making.

Data is not some esoteric phenomenon created by machines and is beyond the comprehension of humans. It is a large puzzle with many solutions and interpretations.

The same thing can be said about data management software. Software is created by teams of people so that it can be used by others. In every software package, there will always be a human logic that can be understood. Often, there are entire teams in software development department that focus on the graphical user interface and customer experience so that their software is user-friendly.

Now that we know that both data and data management software both are heavily influenced by humans, we can begin to feel a bit more comfortable getting our hands dirty and digging right into the thick of these puzzles to extract everything we need.

An important thing we need to keep in mind is that we all make mistakes. We are human! Often, there are mistakes hiding in the data. You may make mistakes analyzing the data. The software you use will freeze and leave you out to dry. It's important to keep a cool head, because this whole process can be extremely frustrating.

There will be times when you see an insurmountable problem solved in a few minutes through the magic of data analysis. There will be other times when the smallest problems take the longest time to solve.

There are a lot of things we can do to make data analysis a lot easier for everyone involved. I will cover these things in this book.

The first point I want to cover is to always be aware of the human factor and try to minimize user error in every way possible. For example, if you have to suggest system qualities, always opt for as many pre-defined fields as possible, over free text. This ensures that whatever data entered is standardized and easy to work with. The other side of this coin would be to understand that free-text user-entered fields are less reliable than automatically collected data or standardized data.

The more human involvement in the data-collection process, the more unreliable the information seems to be due to the statistical probability of errors.

The next biggest human risk involved in data analysis after data-entry errors is the interpretation of data. Misunderstanding what each data point means and where it comes from can cause unreliable results which can lead to unreliable decisions. A period in the wrong place can be the difference between a thousand and ten thousand dollars. Forgetting to use the appropriate units of measure can cause issues down the road when someone who is analyzing the information doesn't have the same assumptions which the person who entered the information had.

An 8x42x12 piece can be either a long thin box or an entire shipping container depending on whether we're talking about inches or feet. A balance sheet will never balance if some of the unlabeled invoices are in euros instead of dollars. This is also the case when a column is labeled "price" but does not specify whether taxes are included.

A different example might be a data column labeled "date" without any specification. We might not be able to distinguish what kind of date this point refers to. While this may be clear to the person entering the data, the person analyzing it may interpret it differently.

Once we have accounted for both types of errors, we can begin to understand the sources of our data. This step should be fairly straightforward. It involves looking at the data columns to understand what pieces of information are available for use. Most columns are self-explanatory, given the context around the data. If you're looking at a purchase order data extract, you can expect things like customer Information, delivery address, products sold, cost, taxes, expected delivery date, etc. If you're looking at manufacturing data, you can expect products, product lines, stages of completion, available-to-promise date, dates relating to each process step, etc.

Depending on the experience level of the analyst and familiarity with the data, it might be necessary to spend some time asking questions to ensure a thorough understanding of the data and the processes from which data points come from before starting any type of analysis. Identifying key players within the organization that might be able to clarify some of the information is highly recommended.

DATA-ORIENTED MINDSET

There might be a million reasons why you might be in the situation where you want to take advantage of the data available to you. But whether you're looking for cost savings, process efficiencies or new business opportunities, the ability to analyze data can go a long way to ensure you make the best decisions using the resources available to you. As with other skilled work, it might help to create a mindset amiable to the type of work ahead. Looking at the data from the point of view of an analyst requires a few key components.

The first component that you need to keep in mind is the understanding of human factors previously mentioned.

The next component needed is the ability to see the data as unbiased as possible. Instead of asking "How can I make the data tell me what I want to hear," ask "What can I the data tell me."

Oftentimes, it is tempting to want to use the information in a way that supports previously held beliefs. We may also want to manicure it so we look good in front of our superiors. Those kinds of practices are not only dishonest, but they can lead to bad decisions that ultimately affect the entire organization. Manipulating the data to tell you what you want is ultimately too easy to do. Be warned though, such shady analytics practices are counterproductive to the spirit of continuous improvement which I promote in this book. What's more, those practices backfire in the long run.

The third component of the data-oriented mindset needed for good data analytics is a good results-oriented outlook. Since data analysis is not such a clear-cut and exact practice, the analyst must be able to take whatever they have and find a way to use it to obtain the results they need. If they need a category, they must be able to create it. If they need a new measurement, they must be able to derive it. If they need more data, they must be able to find out where to get it.

THE IMPORTANCE OF CURIOSITY

Sometimes you dig into the data because you're looking for something specific. You have a question that you're looking for the data to answer. If you approach the data with that mindset, you're sure to eventually find an answer. However, the biggest opportunity with the data isn't in the specific questions you are trying to answer but in exploring the data and finding things you didn't know before. Analyzing data to see what trends and patterns lie underneath often provides an opportunity for improvement. While you're focused on your sales' constant totals, the mix of products might indicate that one of your products is gaining market share and could be capitalized on. Or, while you're looking at the total production totals, you might miss that eliminating the bottleneck between two of your manufacturing processes could increase your total output by 20%.

Of course, those are both theoretical situations and the devil is in the details. But those kinds of opportunities hide underneath the data, waiting to be found. I could write a thousand books on slicing and dicing the data, but none of that would be of any real benefit without the associated mindset that allows for finding those kinds of hidden opportunities. All the tools can get you the answers you're looking for, but this mindset will give you the answers you didn't know to look for.

The same way one would go about finding opportunities, one might also stumble across issues that are hurting or could potentially hurt the business processes the data is representing.

This entire process starts with identifying the issue and then determining what caused it. Sometimes we may not find anything of interest. Other times, we may walk away with something that can be escalated to management who may deem it necessary to do something about it.

THE SCIENTIFIC METHOD

We'll often come across an outlier with many possible different causes. In this case, it's necessary to systematically approach the problem. The best way is the scientific method.

1. Observe
    a. As mentioned above, through your analysis of the data, you come across an outlier.
2. Question
    a. Once the outlier is identified, ask yourself why it might be occurring.
3. Research
    a. If possible, ask a coworker or a source familiar with the data if they know a reason.
4. Hypothesis
    a. If the question persists, formulate a few hypotheses that might be responsible for caus-

ing the data deviations.
5. Experiment
    a. Conduct a few different experiments with the data available to prove or disprove your original hypothesis.
6. Analysis
    a. Analyze the results to establish whether they explain the data deviations. If not, try a new hypothesis.
7. Conclusion
    a. Type a report to be analyzed further and decide if there are any actions that need to be taken.

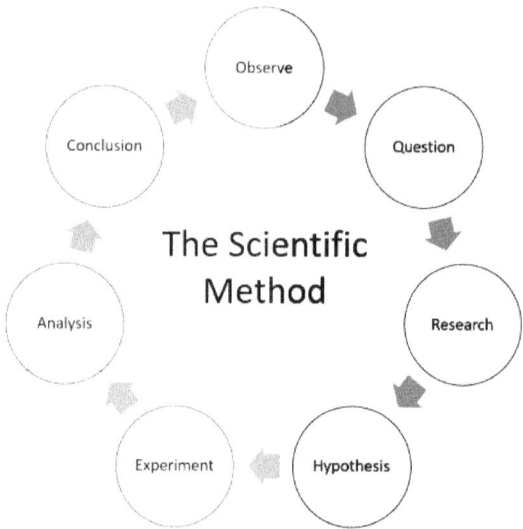

This method of systematic problem-solving is a good example of the kind of knowledge and tools an analyst might need which don't get addressed in the technical books. Tools like this often get neglected as it is assumed that they either don't belong to the field or people already know them. This creates knowledge gaps in any kind of systematic training.

Just like with this systematic approach to data, I highly encourage data analysts to expand their scope and search for new approaches outside of the explicit industry. Using tools outside of the trade often leads to the best results. Approaches such as DMAIC (Define, measure, analyze, implement, control) Agile, and Scrum are also great methodologies for data analysis.

KNOWLEDGE NEEDED

There are four primary knowledge bases which a good analyst can draw from. These areas of knowledge must be actively practiced, sought, and learned.

Analyst Knowlege			
Practical	Technical	General	Industry

1. Practical
    a. This type of knowledge is earned through the experience gained through doing things. As an analyst, it is crucial that you make an active effort to acquire hands-on knowledge of the processes behind the data. This allows you to clearly define and understand where the data is coming from and

how it's collected. You will also understand how the data interacts with other processes or systems and how it is used by the end user.
2. Technical
    a. This is the type of knowledge necessary to perform your job. While it helps you perform your job responsibilities, this knowledge also enables you to continue being marketable in the workplace. Here, you learn about various data analysis systems, from Microsoft Excel right up to more sophisticated methods of data analysis such as Access, Power BI, Tableau, and SQL. This might also include the systems from which you draw the necessary information to do analysis like SAP, Oracle, and any other ERP systems.
3. General
    a. This type of knowledge can help you figure out outside factors that affect the data. For example, a significant drop of export shipments in February could be accounted for by the Chinese New Year. An approaching storm could account for the dramatic spike in revenue

of water, gasoline, and groceries. A corporate restructure could be the reason process times increased in the last quarter.
4. Industry
   a. This type of knowledge will help you understand the data more intimately. Knowing that a motor has different meanings in the automotive and oil industry helps you understand what you're working with. This improves your analysis and conclusions.

ANALYST PROJECT LIFECYCLE

Most data analysis jobs usually fall within two categories.

The first category is reporting analytics. This category focuses on churning out a predetermined set of reports on a regular schedule. Whether they're production reports, spending reports, or steering reports, the analysts ensure that these reports are produced in a timely manner. The results of the projects are then used by other people to do their job. This is the most common category. In my opinion, it is also the biggest underutilization of an analyst's time for a few reasons.

First, these types of reports can be automated and this is my standard recommendation for known long-term business needs. Second, they bring little job fulfillment and security to the analyst. Third, when the inputs and the outputs are known, there is little opportunity for process improvements. This also means an analyst may not have many opportunities to add their biggest value to the company. Finally, these types of reports have terrible manual continuity processes. If an analyst drafting a weekly report is fired and a new one is hired to work on the same report, their assumptions will be different. Therefore, their reports will be different. This causes report variances from one analyst to the other which can harm the integrity of the results in the long run.

The second type of analyst job is the type I'd like to focus on. This is the ad-hoc, project-based, process-improvement, and fact-finding analyst who has goals and the freedom to pursue the answers they need. Included within this category, are people looking for cost savings, process improvements, root causes of different corporate issues, information to support business decisions, and many more. This type of analyst can add the most value to the companies they work for. The analyst must move through the analyst project lifecycle.

The analyst project lifecycle has four stages which will be looking at throughout this book.

DEFINE WORK

The first thing is to try to understand what is being asked of us. For example, if a manager comes down to your office and asks you to find out what we've been spending the most money on, you should have a few questions that narrow down your scope of work, define exactly what you're looking for, and provide you some leads to begin your investigation.

A few questions I would have would be:

1. What do you hope to find out? Controllable expenses? P/L values? Ranked cost per units? Cost per department? Biggest expenses with the smallest returns? Biggest spend leaks?
2. What is the time period you'd like to see? Last year? Last quarter? Last month?
3. What is the area of expenses you need to see? Company-wide? By region? By state? By product families? By product? By department?

All these questions should begin forming a picture in your mind about what the results need to look like. As you ask more and more questions, begin to identify what YOU need to acquire in order to produce the results being asked of you. If your boss is looking to cut costs to make the quarter's end-goals, chances are he's not going to be looking at relocation as a feasible action to save on rent since moving might increase short-term expenses. If you're in the manufacturing environment, chances are your boss isn't going to care about how much the marketing group is spending on advertising. This is likely to be the case even if advertising is the company's overall highest expense.

ACQUIRE DATA

Once you have an idea of what you're looking for, gather your resources and prepare. If you're working with a large company, this may be part of your job training and onboarding process. Getting you access to the right databases and showing you how to access them would the first few steps you take in your new role. If you're a small business owner this step might be more complicated. Depending on the technology available to you, you may have a few options available to you.

Most point-of-sale technologies common to most small businesses have basic data-export capabilities that you can take advantage of. Every time you make a sale, the transaction is recorded, and you have one more point of information. Even learning to use Excel or Access would go a long way to get you analyzing data, and solving problems.

If the technology is beyond your budget, manually capturing the most important details of every transaction might be worth your while as this data might provide you a starting point for your analytics quest. However, I recommend that this only be done temporarily and efforts be made to automate the data-gathering process.

Either way, once you have your project/ questions/parameters defined, arm yourself with the appropriate information so you can start transforming the data.

TRANSFORM DATA

After some data is acquired, the next step is to transform it. This is where data analysis can get a bit tedious. You will often need to transform the data you have into usable data. This could mean sorting, categorizing, organizing, standardizing, etc. before any type of useful insights can be gathered.

If the data is clean enough to draw insights from, this could be a fairly short project where you can easily draw your conclusions.

However, you'll need to clean the data enough to draw preliminary conclusions and then continue cleaning it to answer further questions. You'll need to clean it some more to answer new questions. You'll also need to clean it some more before using it for presentation purposes.

PRESENT INFORMATION

If you're doing data analytics for your own benefit, this could be an unnecessary step for you. When I have questions I'm just hoping to answer for myself, I don't bother with the same show and dance I do if I was answering questions for one of my bosses or clients.

Usually, projects like these have an ending point. Also, you're looking at information to present to your bosses, clients, teachers, board, or to someone that needs it to make decisions. So the data has to be transformed one last time with the purpose of clearly conveying the insights you've drawn so they can be easily understood. This requires trust, credibility, and judgement calls.

From interactive dashboards to regularly scheduled reports, it is crucial to understand the method of communication and the tools available in order to ensure accurate communication of the information. There is nothing worse than spending weeks working on a project and presenting it only to have your bosses make bad decisions because they didn't understand what your conclusions were. Not only does this make for bad business, but you might also be held liable for the results.

MOVING FORWARD

Now that we've covered some of the basics and the underlying themes of data analysis, I'll narrow down the rest of the book and elaborate on some of the points we've briefly touched. This will not only reinforce the points already made, but it will provide a greater understanding of the nuances of each of these steps.

With each new section, I will take you through what each of these steps usually entail. I'll share some personal experiences. I will show you some best practices. I will also highlight some of the most common pitfalls that most analysts encounter.

PART 2: IN THE TRENCHES

NARROWING THE SCOPE

The field of data analysis is growing and with it, the opportunities. If you're reading this, you may already know this. By the time this book is published, the landscape will have changed. So how do you create a piece of work that will endure through to the maturity of the field? Simple. Focus on the essence of data analytics instead of the particularities.

I hope you utilize this book alongside your other resources. On its own, this book will not make you a data analyst. However, utilize it well and it will make you a great one.

The job of an analyst transcends hierarchies because it can be both strategic and tactical. It can be used to make decisions across any planning horizon. Ultimately, it can be used in any size organization.

With the continuous evolution of technology, more and more people have access to data. Often, data analysis is simply a matter of figuring out what to do with this data. Information is no longer a luxury of big companies; it is now a valuable tool to most.

Prior to diving into the technicalities of this chapter, I want to emphasize a point I already made. **Before attempting any data analysis, ensure you understand the project and the scope.**

If your boss meant one thing and you understood another, it will make it very difficult for him to be happy with your results. You might waste a lot of time searching for answers he never cared about while ignoring crucial information he needed. Trust me when I say that having to redo entire projects at the last minute, if it's even possible, is absolutely exhausting.

As a rule of thumb, I always ask as many questions as possible when I'm given new projects. I always take the time to ensure I clarify any ambiguity between myself and the person giving me the project. The answer may be specific. The person assigning the project may "want to look at it quarter-by-quarter and as far back as 2015." You may also be asked to "use your best judgment." Regardless, it's always best to err on the side of caution. It might also be worth your while to run the analysis both ways, just in case.

DATA MINING

Data mining is a particularly important topic because bad information will always give you bad results. The worst part of it is that you might not realize it until the end of your analysis when nothing makes sense. It might not even be noticed until down the line when you're using it for further analysis and you realize that one of the assumptions on which you based everything was wrong and the numbers you've been presenting this entire time are off.

I don't expect you to be able to always tell from the beginning when something like this is happening. However, it is important to acknowledge the possibility and pay due diligence to ensuring you have a good foundation to build upon.

Ensuring you have a good foundation is often a simple task. Depending on the size of the project, the task can turn into a nightmare. For most data analysis projects, you'll probably have one source of data and a few limited answers that you need from it. Using an expense report for a small company to identify where most money is going is a good example. Escalating this task to several expense reports for a big conglomerate with multiple accounting software from all over the world might complicate the entire process.

For the finer technicalities of data mining, I'd refer you to the technical documents and details of whatever software you're trying to extract the information from. From a mindset perspective, here is the first rule of data mining.

ALWAYS START WITH WHAT YOU HAVE

This sounds like a simple rule. However, people who don't have all the information, can be quickly put off if they don't have all the information they need. This is important for various reasons. Even with incomplete information, a person can deduce the underlying patterns well enough to make good decisions. Take into consideration a starting grocery store owner in a developing country with zero technology. No point of sale software. No technology. No computer to keep track of any expenses. How can he use data analysis to better his business?

If your response had anything to do with acquiring technology, you might be missing the entire point of data analysis. The answer to this one is simply to record his transactions. Let's assume that every time someone goes to his store and buys some groceries, he simply writes down what he is selling on a piece of paper.

- ✓ Eggs
- ✓ Milk
- ✓ Eggs
- ✓ Bread
- ✓ Bananas
- ✓ Eggs
- ✓ Milk
- ✓ Bread
- ✓ Eggs
- ✓ Eggs

Based on this list, what can we deduce about his business? While it is a small list without a lot of information, we can see that they seem to be selling mostly eggs. In fact, a quick calculation shows that 50% of the sales are eggs. This simple bit of information can be used to move the business forward. Now that they know this, they might either try to find cheaper eggs or sell them at a slightly higher price depending on their situation. Both of these strategies will undoubtedly increase their profits. Even though they don't have exact numbers, they can decide with a certain degree of accuracy. Perhaps the next level of this would be to ask the grocery store owner to capture two fields: the item and the price he sold them for.

- ✓ Eggs - 2.99
- ✓ Milk - 1.99
- ✓ Eggs - 2.99

- ✓ Bread - 1.99
- ✓ Bananas - 3.99
- ✓ Eggs - 2.99
- ✓ Milk - 1.99
- ✓ Bread - 1.99
- ✓ Eggs - 2.99
- ✓ Eggs - 2.99

With this new set of information and some simple math calculations, we'll discover that eggs are in fact 55% of his total revenue. All he must do now is add in the information about how much he's spending on eggs from his supplier, and we can find out exactly how much profits he'll earn from each case of eggs. If he raises the price or finds cheaper eggs, he'll find out exactly how much that will change his profits in each instance.

Data analysis can get really complex depending on a lot of factors, but it is crucial not to forget the basics. Following our grocery store vendor, let's explore what he had to do to step up his analysis from the first example to the second.

EXPLORE ADJACENT RESOURCES

It will not always be possible to have all the information available to you when you need it. In fact, when it comes to doing things never done before, there's usually an extended period of research necessary before even starting to look at the data. For our grocery store owner, it was simply a matter of finding out from his supplier the purchasing price of the eggs. Perhaps going to the market and shopping around for prices might help him establish some averages that he can use to lower his cost when purchasing eggs. Maybe he can compare his prices to similar grocery vendors in the area. Maybe he can visit the next town to see if things are cheaper there so he can acquire his groceries from that place and secure extra profits.

Let's now move our grocery store 50 years into the future. Let's make it a grocery chain conglomerate and give it operations all over the world. Who would have thought that the small grocery store would come this far?

As a big company divided into different departments, regions, and product lines all with their own systems and processes communicating with each other, finding out how much is spent on eggs is no longer a simple task. The company now has different suppliers all over the world. Each supplier has their own prices as well as transportation, warehousing, and processing costs. They also have their currency exchange rates, import/export tariffs, and state and federal taxes. What this all means is that the same question just became damn near impossible to decipher.

Enter the data analyst for the "eggs department" who's just been hired to work at the company's headquarters in Texas. His mission is simple: find out the total spend on eggs last year, and maintain accurate records for management to make strategic decisions about this product group.

The analyst finds that each geomarket has its own system so he decides he needs to start with the local purchasing data. He takes out everything that is unrelated to eggs and saves his progress. While this could provide a very good answer, it isn't the full picture. For a better picture, he has to find out the cost of transportation of the product. He needs access to the logistics group system. After that, he might go to the facilities group to find out how much it costs them to store the eggs. He might also go to HR to find out how many employees are involved in handling the eggs for the groceries and so on and so forth. He does this until each little piece of the total cost is accounted for.

Depending on management, they might not care about all of that. They might just want the dollar value associated with the purchase of eggs. At that point, our analyst might find the local data and contact each region's manager asking for the equivalent data. When he has done all this, he adds the data up so he can present it to management.

Both approaches to the problem are perfectly acceptable. The only difference lies in what your boss wanted to see. In both instances, he is searching for adjacent sources of data. He is looking for parallel sources that contain the same information for various regions or cross-system data where different pieces of data are scattered across multiple systems.

Looking at the cross-system data, how do we go about mining all the information we need for to find a proper answer?

- ✓ Data-driven approach
    - Find purchasing data on how much was implicitly paid for eggs
        - Purchasing system

- Find out which locations physically acquired the eggs after being purchased
  - Purchasing system
- Find location data
  - Warehouse management system
- Investigate percentage of costs associated with eggs
  - Management knowledge
- Find transportation costs from transportation management system
  - Logistics system
- Repeat for different regions

A different way to visualize this problem and understand it will be to visualize it end-to-end.

- ✓ Visualization approach
  - One egg (cost of actual egg)
  - Fits into a dozen and turns into a stock unit
    - Cost of eggs + packing costs
  - Stock units compile into handling units
    - Stock unit cost + packing costs
  - Handling units compile into shipping units

- Boxed costs + consolidation costs (procurement system)
    - Shipping units compile into truckloads
- Consolidated costs + shipping and handling costs (transportation system)
    - Transport truckload from supplier to warehouse
- Running costs + handling costs + estimated warehousing costs (warehouse system)
    - Warehouse recompiles all units and distributes them to stores
- Running costs + percentage of new transportation costs (transportation system)
    - Stores stock units and sell them to end-client
- Running costs + stocking and handling costs (sales system)
    - Repeat for all regions
    - Account for distinct region-specific costs for each region

Usually, this level of granularity isn't asked for in most reports. However, it is crucial to understand total costs beyond the dollar value associated to purchasing. The vendors will often make everyone's life easier by selling products by the pallet at an all-inclusive cost. This leaves you to only worry about the rest of the calculations. This approach might be better suited for a manufacturing scenario rather than a purchasing scenario. But the point still accurately illustrates all the data points needed to make accurate calculations. This will allow you to find out where all the information is located to begin your search for all the adjacent data flows to complete your picture.

Here is where data analytics starts getting interesting. Once all the sources of information start coming together, connecting them is the next big problem. Software such as PowerBI, Tableau, and various SQL programs has abilities to connect different flows of information using unique values and relational databases. All these programs usually have their own free tutorials, documentation, and plenty of online videos to help you learn them.

There are a lot of technicalities regarding this particular topic, so I'm only going to briefly touch on the basics you might need to get you through the day. But keep in mind that entire college degrees are dedicated to covering all the particulars of this topic in more depth. Having learned a lot of my most useful skills by going at it my own way, I know that there is a lot of information for those with the discipline and the will to seek it out. If you got this book, I assume you are one of the few that have plenty of both.

1. Relational databases

Among various tables and flows of information, there are usually connecting fields that can be used to derive complex information. Focusing on the data fields that connect these different flows can enhance your ability for complex analysis. For example, a table with invoice numbers can be connected to identify exact products if it has references to purchase orders. Purchase order tables can connect to transportation costs if they are tied down to a transportation software by shipment numbers. In ideal situations, all of these are under one system that flawlessly connects them all. But, this is rarely the case.

2. Connecting through assumptions

Through bad organizational planning, some systems of information are broken. If there is a break in information flow where you can't connect two pieces, there are assumptions that can be made. This decreases the accuracy of the data but gives you enough of a connection to get started. For example, if you don't have a direct connection between transportation costs and purchase orders, you can pull daily or weekly totals of both and connect them by averages. A good way to manage the accuracy loss is to regularly revise the averages to ensure they change with the data trends.

DATA CLEANING

"Bad data in. Bad data out" is a very common saying among those who regularly deal with data. As I mentioned earlier, humans make mistakes. Human error is even more common when it comes to repetitive tasks such as data entry.

A common exercise among high school English classes requiring them to "identify the mistakes in a given paragraph" is supposed to teach students how to identify some of the most common mistakes in the language. Now, how do you teach a person to identify mistakes in databases with thousands of different entries? Oftentimes, it is the analyst's job to identify and correct these errors.

While analysts believe it's often impossible to fix every mistake in the data, there is much that can be done to minimize errors. Today's analysts have a broad array of tech tools to clean up data. These include the all-new and groundbreaking artificial intelligence. While these are all nice to have, they are not always accessible or convenient to use. Using artificial intelligence to clean up a spreadsheet of a thousand addresses might be the equivalent of using a sledgehammer to put a nail in a wall.

Regardless of whether you have the sledgehammer or not, I suggest starting with a simple methodology to clean up the data. Here is the already well-known effort/reward matrix.

	Low Effort	**High Effort**
High Reward	Focus on easy wins to gain traction and advance the most in the shortest time.	Decide if it's worth it. Depending on your data sets and your scope, some items may fall in this category. These items might be worth the time/effort investment.
Low Reward	Items in this category can be low-hanging fruit that will move you towards the end-goal easily but also slowly.	Put these off until the end. They are the items that bring diminishing returns for your time/effort.

Using this chart as a starting point of the data-cleaning process can bring a lot of benefits. Most importantly, it provides a good framework by which to ascertain the point at which the data is good enough. Not all questions will need perfect data for them to be answered. In fact, I'd argue that most rarely do. While it would be nice to have perfect data, I know that it's rarely the case in most environments. Everything from misspellings to missing fields to user assumptions can skew the data sets to the point of inaccuracy.

STANDARDIZE

A great first step during any data-cleaning effort is the standardization of known data. For example, when I have to clean large amounts of data in excel, I create a table and sort for common fields. After this, I copy over matching data so it all reads the same way. When working with large amounts of data that need to be standardized, I've found that finding ways to "mass update" information is often a very good start. This is so if the analyst has enough knowledge of the data, permission to make changes and enough confidence in their own judgement calls.

Take, for example, a recent exercise I did where I had to clean up manually entered U.S addresses for a year's worth of transactional records. Starting with the states, I took every version of each state and standardized it into one version. I filtered the state column to show me "Texas", "TX", "TX,", "TX.", "Tex", etc. and changed them all for the widely recognized state code "TX". These were some of the easiest mistakes to fix and recognize and would help me accurately measure the number of transactions by state.

Once I accomplished the first task, I figured standardizing cities would be a good next step since there were only a handful of cities in each state in which our facilities were located. Again, I went state by state and looked for all the duplicate records I could find. I found 11 different spellings of Houston. These included "Hoston", "Houston", "Huston", "Housto", "Houston." and "Houfston".

Once I finished, I started looking at the companies themselves. I found about two to three different versions of some of the companies and standardized them by using their legal name or common version of the name.

It's also important to mention that I briefly considered double-checking each of the records against a different system. I wanted to make sure all the item numbers in the transaction data matched each of the items in each transaction. I decided that this wouldn't be worth it since it was extremely time-consuming, and it would bring little to no contribution to the final scope of the questions I needed to answer. Perhaps on a different project where each item numbers held a higher priority, exploring this avenue might have been worth the time and effort.

CATEGORIZE

After we've taken the data and cleaned it up a bit, we can begin categorizing it. Categorizing is important so we can begin to form trends and patterns from scattered data. If your overall expenses are going up, categorizing your information might help you figure out if there is a specific demographic or segment that needs attention. Once these trends are recognized and isolated, we can begin to make intelligent decisions.

Take, for example, an automobile manufacturer that keeps track of all the service issues they handle. Looking at the entire list, you might see thousands of different issues. Depending on the size of the dealership, it might be a huge set of information to dig through and make sense of.

On this project, I might focus on creating a few different categorization schemes to understand the issues. One of these schemes might be related to the cost of fixing the issues. I'd create low, medium, and high cost tiers. Furthermore, I'd classify the types of issues into buckets such as mechanical, electrical, and cosmetic.

If those buckets aren't enough to give me any insights into what might be causing this, I might go further down and narrow the classifications. I'd classify the data into things like engine/oil, drive belts, power steering, radiator/heater/hoses, battery/cables, brakes, tires, lights, instruments, etc.

A new category I might add after narrowing the issue classifications might be whether the part that caused the issue is from an in-house department or it was brought from an external supplier. It might be revealed that a supplier has a high failure rate that could be hurting our final product. In this case, we will need to consider other options.

FOCUS ON WHAT YOU NEED

As I have previously mentioned, it will be impossible to always get perfect data. Furthermore, usually when people ask for answers, they don't have weeks to wait for data to be perfectly clean before they get a response. This is when it becomes crucial to prioritize, so that we don't spend any unnecessary time working on data that won't advance us towards finding the answers we need.

A good way to narrow down your focus is simply to take a bit of time to prepare yourself before you start analyzing the data. When it comes to big data sets, I try to identify underlying "formulas" that will help me find the answers I need.

For example, if I'm looking at a set of data to see where we are spending the most money, I can use the following variables to find the answer I need: monetary values and categorization scheme. I'd first standardize or clean the monetary values as far as converting the funds to a common currency. Then I'd decide if this answer warrants a geographical approach, in which case I'd focus on finding and cleaning the geographical data to ensure its accuracy. If the answer requires a categorical approach based on a set of predetermined values, I'd standardize the data into those values to produce a cohesive and accurate answer.

Similarly, if I need to determine the demand of each product family in each region, I would make sure the product families and regions are properly categorized before starting any analysis on quantities. When we want to know this demand, we can deduce the next set of questions that might be asked and try to get ahead of the requests. One of the possible follow-up questions is usually related to money. How much product demand is there, and what is the equivalent dollar value? High product demand for a low-profit item might not be as important as low product demand for high-profit Items, depending on their respective quantitative analysis.

Ultimately, narrowing down to what you need will allow you to prioritize. But don't forget to keep continuity in mind. For example, write down your assumptions so you can replicate the report with the same assumptions in the future. If, in your first report, you categorize computers under entertainment expenses and in the next report, you categorize them as work expenses, the two reports will be inconsistent and inaccurate. This will likely lead to bad decision-making.

As a general practice, when I work on data projects, I keep a running tally of assumptions and results on a summary page. I do this in case I have to revisit the project after a long break or need to share my work with anyone who will be able to see my rationale behind my decisions.

WORKING ACROSS SYSTEMS

The higher you move up in an organization, the higher the chances your daily work is spread out among various systems. Your company might have all the contracts on one system and the client information on a different one. The vendor information could be on another system while manufacturing uses its own system. The finance department might also have a few of its own systems. What this all does is create huge internal rifts in communication that can be very difficult to overcome.

While businesses everywhere are realizing that communication across systems oftentimes brings multiple issues, it will take a long time before the bulk of companies move to a single system for all the processes. Even when they do, there will be a steep learning curve to figure out all the quirks.

In the meantime, it is crucial to understand how information flows from one system to another before attempting to put them together. For example, if you have your billing information in one system and your operations in another, find all the information that transfers overs so you can understand the limitations and the connections that you will have to make in order to make sense of the data.

Since systems are usually designed around different organizational functions, the people creating the systems usually do not bother bringing in information from other systems which the system does not need. The full supply-chain picture is often scattered across multiple systems and difficult to piece together. Sometimes the information is not going to be on your systems, and you must go to a different system to find the answers you need. However, that doesn't prevent the need to look for answers that span over multiple systems. It's usually up to the analyst to piece together all they need from different systems so effective business decisions can be made.

Depending on the size of the company and the scope of the questions, this might range from "mildly annoying" to "impossible to do alone." While I can't give you a blueprint to address every situation, I can give you some guidelines to get you started.

Start with your inputs and outputs.

Whether you're a small business or a big enterprise, information came from somewhere, and it's going somewhere. Sometimes it's the department down the hall or your supplier across the city. Identifying these points could help you find a lead by which to investigate the supply chain until you have all the information you need to answer any questions.

One of the most useful set of skills regarding data analysis are the soft skills. Email requests can only get you so far but personally knowing people that can bridge gaps between systems and clarify things for you will go a long way in enriching your decision-making and data-analysis abilities. This often means spending extra time getting to know people on a personal level, doing favors for them and maintaining open lines of communication that can jumpstart your thinking or challenge your assumptions when you're looking at the data.

You will also need is to learn how to conduct proper research. This will be one of your most invaluable skill as an analyst, particularly when you're asked to bring outside assumptions or discover and quantify things that haven't been explored before. I recommend continuous education, lots of online DIY videos, and lots of books.

TARGETED DATA-FINDING

Most of the time someone needs to look at data for whatever reason, it's not exploratory but targeted exploration. The problem most analysts face when they have complex but specific problems is how to take the raw data and turn it into the answers they need in a way they want to present it. This takes careful planning and a little bit of wit, but it's rarely an unsolvable problem.

REASON BACKWARDS

When it comes down to extracting specific answers from the data, you usually have multiple levels of analysis you need to undergo before getting your final answers. Most times, executives want a single number or metric to explain or summarize thousands of lines of data. Depending on the case, they might want a whole dashboard to look at complex issues from different sides.

Usually the methodology is similar. Reason backwards and aggregate necessary values. If you want to measure profits or losses over time, you need revenue, expenses, and cost of goods sold. From the end-goal, we've extrapolated primary goals we need to solve. Looking at revenue as an example, we might see a new set of problems, such as currency, geo markets, and profit centers. Expenses might come with problems of depreciation and interests. Cost of goods sold might come with issues of reconciling variable costs of inventory over time as well as factoring in warehousing and transportation. The answer often takes just one level of extrapolation, but others might have multiple levels before you have anything you can reasonably extract from the raw data.

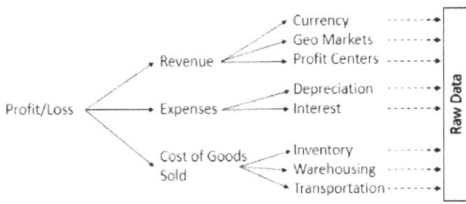

Ultimately, the point of this methodology is to start with the ultimate goal in mind and reason backwards. Identify all the points of information you need to go from the raw state to the end state. This helps you see the comprehensive plan that will transform the raw data into the answers you're looking for. Once this is set, it's just a matter of working on the problems one by one.

CONNECT TO THE BIGGER PICTURE

Whether it was your plan or someone else's, it's important to keep the end-goal in mind. Perhaps in the grand scheme of things, you're only responsible for a smaller portion of the analysis and that your managers will decide to roll up into their own analysis. In most cases, there's a person responsible for each of the data points that lead to the company's end-goals. Understanding these goals and where you stand in the information chain can be useful in the overall improvement of the data chain.

Where the end-goal of your chain of reports is to understand expenses and your portion surrounds the transportation expenses, do you consider overnight hotel stays for the carrier's drivers as part of the transportation cost? The nuances of this question will sway the answer either way. If you're looking for the total cost of transportation, an expense like this should be included. However, if your bosses are wanting the information to understand how the exact costs are broken down so they can attempt to influence it, it might not matter as much to them. If you don't know something like this, you can leave the information for them to look at it whichever way they choose. You can note the assumptions that went into that particular number or have a cost breakdown available for further analysis.

Whether known or not, the end-goal has a subtle influence on the assumptions and nuances of the analysis. Only by looking at the chain of commands and understanding their driving influences, can we provide answers to questions not asked but worth knowing.

CUTTING UP THE QUESTIONS

Alongside this line of thinking, is the issue of finding answers to specific questions and trying to figure out how best to portray the information so it's easy to digest. Let's say you work for a company that manufactures wooden furniture. If your analysis of the spend data involves looking at only two raw materials (say, wood and metals), would it surprise anyone if wood accounts for 90% of the expenses? This probably wouldn't make a good analysis, even though your numbers might be perfectly sound.

A more useful analysis would be if we cut up the wood into different product categories. These categories can be oak, pine, maple, cedar, etc. Metal could be categorized into nails, hinges, screws, etc. The level of analysis would be a lot more useful for someone trying to cut costs or boost profits.

The main benefit of cutting up the question in different ways is avoiding presenting data in ways that are not helpful. Ultimately, the data should be helping people make educated data-driven decisions. If your data doesn't enable that, you should look for other ways to analyze it so that it can.

CALCULATED AND DERIVED DATA

When working with information, there will inevitably come a point where the raw data is there, but you must make calculations between data fields in order to make it meaningful. Depending on the type of data you're working with, there will be a lot you can do and a lot you can't. For example, a common type of calculation in business is the difference between two dates. This is particularly useful to identify and measure how much time things take. If you're working in transportation, knowing this can help you provide more accurate deliver-by dates to your customers. If you're working in manufacturing, you can identify where the most time is being wasted on activities that don't add value.

Take for example a manufacturing process like the one mentioned above. Data may show you that it takes a total of three days or 72 hours to convert raw material into finished goods. You also realize that the processing time for each of the five machines data must go through averages about an hour each. In this case, what is the material doing during the other 67 hours? This may seem like an exaggerated example, but it is a lot closer to reality than you might realize. In those 67 extra hours, the material is usually being transported from one place to another or waiting in queues as work-in-progress.

As an executive for such a company, it might be worth some money to understand how we can cut down those 67 hours and process items faster while enhance our production capabilities. As silly as it may sound, the whole thing may be reduced by moving the machines closer together. It's also a common issue in instances like these that one of the five machines might be bottlenecking the entire process. Buying another machine might exponentially reduce downtime.

UNDERSTANDING ASSUMPTIONS

Assumptions are a big concern when it comes to data handling. Which is why it's often necessary to have a person who is intimately familiar with the processes that produce the data. When you see a price, does it include or exclude taxes? When you see a date, is it manually or automatically captured? At what specific point of the process is the date captured? When you see a weight on an item, is it total weight, total product weight, or total packaged weight? When you see a shipment completion time, what does it include? What does it exclude?

All these seemingly minor nuances of the data can affect the metrics you use to make your decisions. This makes it harder to make accurate decisions if you don't understand the underlying processes and how they connect to the data, particularly when it's time to use the data to make new calculations.

After gathering meticulous data, you find that on average it takes 15 minutes from the time a customer enters the door to the time they walk out. Do you think the level of satisfaction will be the same if they spend three of those 15 minutes waiting in line vs. spending 12 of those minutes waiting in line?

If "start time" in your data is the time the client enters your bank, but the analyst looking at the information believes it is when the client starts transacting with the teller and this information is passed on, you might be in trouble with corporate for having ridiculously slow transaction times compared with the other branches. Both of you will be looking at the same numbers, but you will believe different things from them. While your transacting time might stand at four minutes per transaction, your corporate will believe they're taking you 15 minutes per transaction.

If your corporate headquarters uses these numbers to calculate how many people your tellers service per hour, they might make decisions believing your tellers can only service four people per hour. Meanwhile, the tellers can actually service about 15 people per hour. If your corporate headquarters originally asked these questions to decide which of the local branches to cut, this misunderstanding in the data might cost some people their jobs.

Understanding the assumptions is crucial to understanding the information. However, misunderstood assumptions can be dangerous once they start blending with other fields to produce the calculations by which the business is run. Once this happens, you might not be able to see or understand why your numbers are skewed.

START WITH UNIVERSAL CALCULATIONS

Once you realize that the only way to get the information you need from the information you have is to manually calculate some fields, it's worth having some general knowledge of some universal calculations.

The first two types of calculations that everyone understands are total values and averages. Total values are calculated by adding all the values in a common set of fields. Averages which are calculated by adding all the values together and diving it by the number of total values.

Concrete calculations like these make it easy to begin understanding the data. Adding all the values in each category will give you great points of comparison between your categories. Average costs will help you put single numbers to items with small variability which you can then compare against other categories of averages. I speak about these two calculations because they are important foundations for meaningful analysis. Whether you're the CEO of a huge corporation or a small shopkeeper, totals and averages are two ways that will help you understand the majority of data. These two calculations alone can push a business forward if used diligently and cleverly.

As businesses grow and evolve, they begin to adopt more sophisticated sets of data. They will want a broader variety of metrics by which to run their businesses.

Certain formulas become crucial for making sophisticated business decisions. These include:

- Net income [income - expenses]
- Cost of goods sold [beginning inventory value + purchases of inventory - ending inventory value]
- Gross profit [sales – cost of goods sold + gross profit]
- Gross profit margin [gross profit ÷ sales]
- Break-even point [fixed costs ÷ (sales price per unit – variable costs per unit)]

These calculations form the basis of a "common language" by which business leaders can make decisions. Most of these formulas are taught in business schools. However, the information is widely available in the internet for those willing to learn.

    Only when these types of calculations are not enough, is it recommended to creatively use the data to create new calculations or measures by which to make decisions.

CUSTOM CALCULATIONS

As an analyst, you will often be asked to evaluate things that aren't exactly easy to measure. This is the point where you have to think outside of the box. You will need to get adjacent metrics, make some assumptions, and create new measurements by which you can make decisions. These custom calculations are the types of calculations that require the most thought and caution.

Let's pretend you get hired as an analyst consultant to improve workplace productivity for a book editing company. How do you measure productivity? Could you use mistakes fixed per hour? If the company gets a good writer, it might look like it's not doing much. Could you use book pages read? Staff might end up speed-reading through everything without understanding what they need from the text. Could you use projects finished per week? This would ignore the fact that some projects take significantly longer than other projects. So as an analyst, what exactly can you do?

After some conversations with management and the team, you decide to come up with your own grading scale for the team of editors. Since all the manuscripts are requested in a standardized format, you apply the following logic to evaluate productivity in the workplace.

Criteria	Logic	Weight
Monthly Book Turnover Rate	Books accepted divided by books completed per month	50%
Editing Page Ranking	% of pages edited monthly divided by total monthly department pages edited	20%
Query Letters Reviewed	% of queries reviewed that arrive to inbox divided by total queries	10%
Book Success Ranking	% of monthly books sold divided by company total monthly	20%
	Productivity Score	

Based on this ranking you invented for the project, you create custom scores for each one of the editors based on metrics that are easily tracked. These metrics include projects accepted, projects completed, pages in each project, incoming queries, queries reviewed, and total books sold.

The numbers alone mean absolutely nothing to anyone outside of the company. The custom calculation comes from internal metrics and agreements with company management. The metrics and rankings serve as a guide for management to make data-driven, personnel decisions regarding bonuses, layoffs, or promotions.

These types of custom calculations can often serve to quantify work and make decisions. However, the calculations are often flawed and should be used sparingly and as a last resort. When they are implemented, they should be communicated as explicitly and widely as possible. They should also include the logic that went into each of the metrics.

ASSUMPTIONS AND RISKS OF CUSTOM CALCULATIONS

Many people have the astounding ability to turn great ideas into poorly executed plans. These can be for a plethora of reasons, but the one I see the most often is the lack of foresight. People often forget that actions have reactions. Those actions are particularly troublesome when information is not effectively communicated to all the stakeholders and the metrics implemented to make good decisions end up hurting the company in the long run.

Take the previous example and analyze it for a bit. Before deciding to make a custom calculation final, I have two tests that it must pass before I decide to implement it.

1. How do I cheat this system?

2. How can this go wrong?

Implementing calculations like these often brings along unintended consequences. This is why it's often necessary to play the devil's advocate with your own plan. Doing it systematically is an even better way to ensure that you don't not accidentally make a terrible decision. This is the trial-by-fire. I set up a beautiful plan, and I let a few people listen to it as it is written and then tear it to shreds.

Let us go back to the book editing company we mentioned earlier. In the grading scale, the first criteria is the monthly book turnover rate, which is books accepted divided by books completed per month. Furthermore, let us assume that this had been the only measure we put in place. A lazy employee might decide to just accept one easy project per month and leisurely enjoy a 100% metric. Productive employees who push themselves with multiple projects could fall short and end up penalized if they accidentally take on more than they can finish.

This type of implementation might lead hardworking employees to start doing the bare minimum because it is better for their scores and ultimately their self-interest.

If on that same example, If I would have implemented the second criteria since it seemed a lot easier to track, I could have accidentally given an unfair advantage to employees who excel at grammar and book editing but lack the other attributes that make good book editors.

These criteria alone might have the adverse effect of costing the company good employees who will leave for other companies that will recognize their talents.

Looking at these two examples, it would be easy to see how any of these criteria would adversely damage the company instead of helping executives make good decisions. A matrix such as the one suggested earlier might take away some of the accidental adverse effects. It might provide a fair playing field in which the self-interests of the editors are in line with the interests of the company.

The suggested matrix is by no means perfect. Depending on the priorities of each company, there might be new metrics or different weights to measure performance. However, they should never be implemented lightly or haphazardly. Also, they should always get tested for negative impacts.

DEEP DIVE

There are times when a set of seemingly unrelated data will start presenting the same symptoms, and you'll have to find out if it's a simple technological glitch or a broader problem. Other times, a pattern that you have noticed gives you a glimpse of an opportunity that might be hiding beneath the processes. This is when it becomes necessary to deep dive into the data and find the root causes.

As data grows and becomes more complex, deep dives become more important in data analysis. The further the decision-making point is from the transactional data, the less visibility there is from the top down. This way, it's easier to miss problems and opportunities. This is where data analysts and data-oriented managers can shine above the rest of the employees.

Deep dives are not always simple. They require a high amount of focus, attention to detail, and even deductive reasoning. Still, they can be incredibly beneficial. The most important thing to keep in mind regarding deep dives is the importance of prioritizing things. Deep dives are often time-consuming and will usually narrow down the scope to very small sample sizes. This is why it is important to keep in mind what you're hoping to gain from it, and focus on the deep dives that bring you the most benefit.

Consider the next two problems. The first is a subset of orders that haven't been transferred from the manufacturing system to the logistics system. The second problem is a subset of orders that have invoicing errors which are preventing payments from being be received. Which of these problems should take priority?

A preliminary analysis should give you an answer. In an ideal world, you'd have the IT team working on one problem while the invoicing team works on the other one. This isn't always an option. You will often have to choose where to spend your efforts.

Some of the considerations you should be looking for are as follows:

1. Subsets of orders impacted
2. Value of subsets
3. Your level of access
4. Your controls over each process
5. Complexity of the problem
6. Risk level of the issue

A problem with a single order worth a million dollars might take precedence over 200 orders worth 50 dollars each. With two problems worth a million dollars each, do you first work on the issue you have more control or leverage over, or the one which will take the shortest amount of time to fix? Do you first work on the problem that can bring you the biggest long-term issues, if not fixed immediately?

There will never be an easy answer to things like these. Individual judgement should also be of outmost importance when it comes to making these types of decisions. Depending on your personality, skill, and standard risks of work, all of these judgement calls will shape the decisions you make, and the effect they have on the company.

Here's a good starting point for those unsure of their judgement when it comes to deep dives. The chart is based on two parameters—control and impact—and should help one with their decisions.

High Control/ High Negative Impact	High Control/ Low Negative Impact	High Control / Low Positive Impact	High Control / High Positive Impact
Work Immediately	Work as Possible	Work as Possible	Work as Priority
Low Control / High Negative Impact	Low Control / Low Negative Impact	Low Control / Low Positive Impact	Low Control / High Positive Impact
Escalate Immediately	Monitor	Last Priority	Prepare Proposal for Escalation

The chart should be self-explanatory but the logic behind it may not be. The underlying goal of most companies isn't exactly to make money but to continue making money. This implies the need to secure the survival of the company first then thrive.

Given this outlook, anything that threatens the survival of the company should be addressed immediately. Depending on your level of control, it would be your job to either raise the red flags to the appropriate parties or begin working on fixing these potentially catastrophic situations.

Low impact findings could range between incremental improvements, and mildly annoying problems. These findings will not be lifechanging, but they can help bring projects to slowly better the company's day-to-day. When working these low impact findings, I recommend giving priority to issues you have the most control over.

Situations where you do not have much control and do not have a strong impact should be monitored regularly, but it does not pay to focus too much on them.

I believe positive high-impact situations should always be made a priority. This is particularly important in cases where there is nothing catastrophic around the corner. If it's within your control, these situations should be continuously worked through. If it's not within your control, a thorough improvement plan should be put together. This plan should clearly outline the impact of the positive change while suggesting a plan of action.

FINDING OUTLIERS

Now that we covered how deep dives should be prioritized, let's focus on learning how to identify them as they are often hard to see.

Outliers are points or sets of data that fall outside the normal measurements. These might include spending too much money on a category that shouldn't be so expensive. Things taking significantly longer than they should or quality failures of most sorts are other examples.

The first rule of thumb is that anything that catches your eye should be considered for a possible deep dive. It's often the case that we find something odd that could potentially lead to further insight. Most experienced professionals can easily spot patterns when it comes to the information they're familiar with. This is why it's important that as a generalist, you try to understand the data as intimately as possible before analyzing it. As a specialist, you need to develop your skills in data analytics so that you can use them to discover insights.

As a professional, you'll often come across an issue you think could be vastly improved. This is when a deep dive might come in handy. It allows you to look at the data more closely. What's more, you're able to take away specific examples and present the data to decision makers who could help you optimize the process.

Say you think your organization is spending too much money on a subset of items such as disposables. You ask for some data and find out that you're spending a few hundred dollars on a monthly basis. So, you deep dive into the data and find that the bulk of those disposables are the plastic cups everyone uses in the break room to get water or coffee. For the cost of a month's worth of cups, you could get everyone at the office a set of reusable mugs. This would drastically bring down the cost of the disposables in the long run. You might still need a few disposables for guests. Still, what used to be a month's worth of cups is now three or four months' worth. The outliers in this situation are discovered by looking more closely at the set of data "Disposables" for a common pattern "Cups" which leads to an overall improvement.

This example is quite simple, but it illustrates that the insights don't always have to be generated from the data. They can come from the analyst, and the data can provide the details necessary to make meaningful decisions.

Let's assume you're now looking at a different set of data. You notice that the estimated time to deliver an order from your warehouse to any destination is 30 days. According to your data, you only deliver 80% of those orders within those 30 days. What would you suppose the late orders have in common?

There could be several underlying problems here. The system parameters for how much delivery time should take could be wrong. There could be a shortage of transportation in the industry. The logistics dispatcher could have been missing all the orders coming via email instead of through the proper systems. A deeper investigation of the issue will ascertain what the root cause of the problem is. It will also enable you to determine and propose possible solutions.

If outliers are still not clear, there are multiple processes that we could look at and make them stand out.

Grouping and quantifying is a good way to identify outliers. By grouping the data into buckets and categories, we can begin to identify quantities associated with them and try to understand all the pieces that go into it. In large data sets, it's useful to try to group and quantify data in as many ways as needed until the patterns become clear.

Business analytics software might be able to help narrow down the time to gain those insights, but it's not always necessary.

Analyzing historical data can also be a great way to establish a baseline and some context by which you judge your measurements and results. If you've spent an average of $100 on your electricity bill and this month you spent $200, this may point out that something happened that kicked the common systems out of control and cost you additional money. However, if your monthly electricity costs usually vary between $100 and $300 dollars, the same $200 would fall within the expected costs. Thus, it will not point towards any bigger issue. Any sudden shifts in the data would indicate that a deep dive is necessary to find the root cause.

Benchmarking against third-party data can also be a great method of finding outliers. For example, after running all your calculations, you realize that you are spending on average five dollars per mile on transportation. You can compare this with various sources of information out there to see where other similar companies stand in relation to you. If your primary competitor is paying four dollars per mile on transportation, this could point to a major disadvantage that you need to address in order to stay competitive. After this, you might decide to deep dive into the data and figure out exactly where that extra dollar is going.

DATA HIERARCHIES

Depending on your current data structure and how high you are in the organization, you might have some additional challenges to overcome. One of the biggest challenges is understanding the way the data transforms and moves up and down the hierarchy. As data rolls up higher and higher, it might lose or change some of its meaning. Take manufacturing data for a big organization, for example. Weekly, each manufacturing plant consolidates the information on whatever products they're responsible for that were produced that week. The workers on the ground floor have to aggregate all their work and report to their line managers. The line manager report this to the building managers who report to the sub-region manager who reports to the region manager who reports to the vice presidents.

These pyramids of information often don't have smoothly flowing data. This may lead to a big game of telephone. If the corporate culture isn't one that enforces accuracy either through systems or processes, the data that arrives at the top might be skewed one way or another.

For example, the bonus for one of the floor managers in the above scenario is attached to the performance of their team. If their numbers are not met, the manager might be tempted to inflate his numbers and safeguard his bonus. At that point, the entire chain will have inaccurate data. In the case where this information isn't conveyed through reports but through system data, the opportunity to cheat the system is significantly reduced. Where data has to switch systems, this potentially leaves breaks in the communication lines that can be taken advantage of by whomever has opportunity and stake. Again, this reduces data reliability at each step. Even if the misreporting of information isn't done on purpose, each of the people involved in the data pyramid add a certain margin of error that could accumulate into bad decisions.

At the lowest level of the reporting, you can get granularity down to the line item that was produced, what part numbers went into each completed product, and how much time and effort went into each unit. However, at the highest levels, all you see are aggregated product and region numbers. The higher up you look at the data from, the more it becomes "smooth" due to all the assumptions and judgement calls made along the way.

Therefore, it is crucial to always understand where you stand on the data pyramid and make an active effort to validate every input that leads to the information before it ever reaches your hands. The more bad data that slips through the cracks at the bottom of the chain, the worse the data that arrives at the top.

One of the quickest tests of the information is simply mapping out the aggregations that the data went through from the single point of origin to the aggregate report that arrived at your hands.

ROOT CAUSE ANALYSIS

Ultimately, the purpose of the deep dives is simple: to gain insights. For problems, this means finding their root cause. Once you drill down into the data you, will eventually find the line that separates it from processes. This is your cue to jump off the computer and take a deeper look at the processes themselves.

For example, after all your analysis, you discover that a step in your process is bottlenecking things. It might be useful to walk down to your shop and investigate what exactly is causing this bottleneck. Perhaps you need more machines. Maybe you're missing the personnel to run these machines more efficiently. Perhaps the materials necessary to run the machine continuously get stocked out and this creates massive delays in your process.

Whatever the root cause is, finding it should be the outmost priority as it will give you a clear insight into which steps you or your company should be taking next. Sometimes the root causes will be clear. Other times, even after diving as far as the data goes, the root cause of the problem won't be as easy to spot. If you ever reach this point, check your parameters. Check your processes. Check your people.

Sometimes the data will only tell you "what" is happening instead of "why" it is happening. This is when you must take a more commonsense approach to your analysis and explore outside the data. Subject matter experts are usually a great resource when you get to this point of the data analysis. Take your data and your findings and use them to start a meaningful conversation with the people at the center of these processes. Asking for their input is usually all that is needed to understand the root causes. Chances are high that they have noticed what is happening and might have some ideas as to how to make it better.

There are some lean tools that also make it easier to find root causes outside the data. While I won't go over all of them, I will highlight the ones I've found the most useful throughout my career. I also highly recommend diligently studying Six Sigma and Lean methodologies as they can provide many tools and insights.

FIVE WHYS

The Five Whys is probably the most useful method I've found when trying to establish the root cause of various issues. The concept is quite simple and self-explanatory. You repeatedly ask yourself "why" until you find the root cause of any issue.

For example, your data reveals that one of your warehouses has the highest amounts of returns. The first thing you do is ask yourself "why." After enough investigation, you discover that the warehouse has a higher percentage of items that are damaged in transit. You ask yourself "why" this is the case. The question often leads to an answer via deductive reasoning. There are times when you will need to analyze your data some more. To answer the second "why," let's say the warehouse has the oldest delivery vans in the company's fleet. Shock absorption is terrible and this is leading to so many items breaking during transit.

This leads to a crossroads in decision making depending on break-even analysis and cost estimations. If there's enough money and it's time for an upgrade, we can show that money invested in getting a new delivery truck will pay off in the long term in both service quality and decreased breakages. Another solution might be to replace or upgrade the shock systems in all the vehicles.

After looking at the shock systems in your fleet, you realize that it wasn't as old as you previously thought. This means the shock system isn't a cause for all the in-transit damage. This also means you continue to ask yourself "why." After more investigation, you realize that all the drivers for the warehouse have been at the company for less than six months. You look at their training records and see that all of them are working but didn't finish their on-the-job training. When you ask "why" this is the case, you find out that it's because middle management isn't enforcing the training requirements set forth by the company's leadership.

You realize that you might have hit the root cause of the issue. Without proper training and procedures, products are highly likely to be damaged during transit. Knowing this, it might seem like a good place to stop investigating and simply spend the necessary money and time to get them all trained.

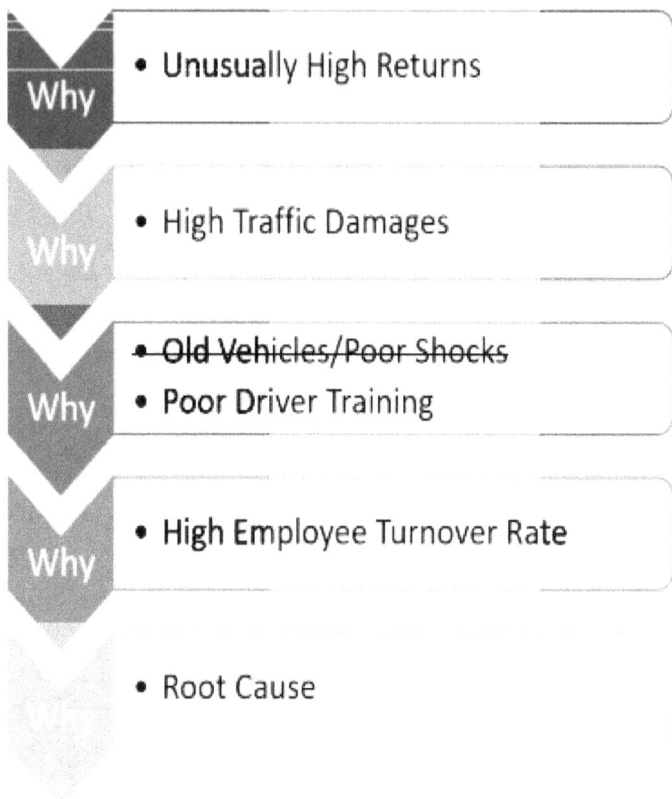

Be warned though, always look for other possible causes because you might walk away thinking the problem is solved only to be dragged back to it later. If you look at this problem more carefully, it might become clear that this isn't a training issue but a turnover issue. Employees come and go too quickly. Therefore, they are always behind. New employees are under a lot of pressure to perform. Unsurprisingly, there is never any time for them to complete their training.

Ensuring that training is completed might be a short-term solution since the employees might not last long at the company. Asking "why" might lead you to understand the reasons for the company's high turnover rates. This will lead you onto a strong resolution to your problem. Addressing the turnover rates will lead to more experienced and properly trained drivers. This will lead to higher quality of delivery to the end customer.

FISHBONE DIAGRAM

The next of my favorite root cause analysis tools is the Ishikawa diagram. Also known as the fishbone diagram, this tool focuses on cause and effects. I use it when I come across a complex problem that could have various root causes. Combining this tool with data analysis often results in a list of root causes with various corresponding impacts that could lead to decisions by management which are based on the priorities of the company.

The process for creating a fishbone diagram is quite simple. (Insert Picture)

At the far right, you write up the main issue and draw a line from it towards the left. From this line, you create branches focused on various categories that might lead to the problem. And from those branches, you create more branches of root causes that lead to that category of issues.

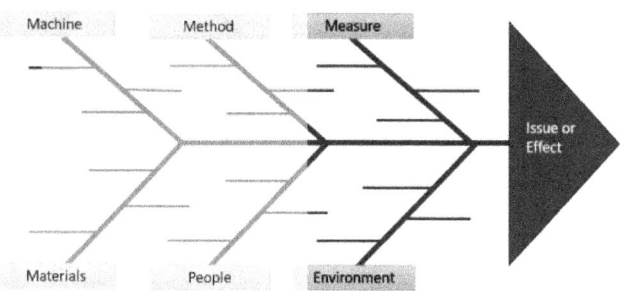

The categories may vary depending on the type of problem and estimated causes that may lead up to the primary issue. Still, it is important to look at all the possible categories that may influence the outcomes so you can properly ascertain what causes problem, what the impact of the problem is.

Using the same company from the previous example let us explore a different problem. Let us assume that a large percentage of the deliveries has been arriving late. The categories that we could investigate could be:

1. People: Are the drivers responsible?
    a. If so, what are the reasons?
2. Are the vehicles responsible?
    a. If so, why?
3. Are the materials responsible?
    a. How so?
4. Is the environment responsible?
    a. How so?

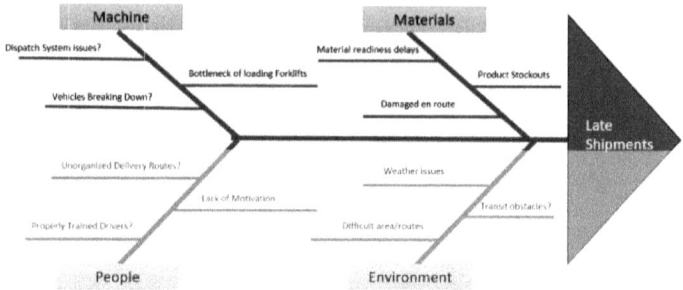

After this exercise, you can take your analysis to the next logical level: evaluating all the causes and quantifying them. For example, how many drivers have completed all their required training? how many years of experience does each driver have? what is the total mileage of the route they drive? what is their average completion time? how many incidences are there where the material isn't finished on time? how often do vehicles break down?

For all those quantifiable questions, proper data analysis would be needed to derive real actionable decisions that address the problems.

THE SCIENTIFIC METHOD

If there is not much of a visible root cause or a way to discern it, the next best available methodology is the good old-fashioned scientific method. Using experience and gut feelings, the scientific method is the perfect approach to shot-in-the-dark root cause finding. As a method of exploration into the cause of data-related findings, it is methodical, replicable, standardized, and easy to keep track.

After digging in with one theory, the results will often lead you to a new insight. You can use the new insights to further probe the data. This exploratory road can ultimately lead you to the root cause of multiple issues. However, it might take a lot more work and may take longer to show results compared to targeted data-finding.

REPORTING

Analyzing data for your own purposes comes with definite freedom of action that isn't usually experienced by most data analysts. These analysts work for different size businesses and corporations. Their single job is to make sense of the data and explain it to the people that have to make the decisions. Analysts translate computer-generated outputs into human-friendly inputs such as explanations, reports, and presentations.

Day after day, lots of great ideas go unnoticed because the person they were presented to did not understand them. This is tragic for the individual spending all their time building up a great idea and doing all the leg work. It's also tragic for the world that might miss out on a great industry-changing idea because the person who discovered the idea, was shot down by the person in management that didn't understand it.

I want to dedicate the rest of the book to turning great insights into coherent human-friendly presentations that will ensure those ideas get the attention they deserve. You will be able to identify your success if whomever you are presenting to commends your presentation or asks for your recommendations.

    Data creates knowledge, but knowledge on its own is not power. Knowledge applied into action towards a specific goal is power. Knowledge provides the mechanism. Action provides the energy to move. The goal provides the direction to take. Without all three, data analysis is simply glorified theoretical questions from a fancy source.

KNOW YOUR AUDIENCE

The most crucial advice regarding any type of presentation is to know your audience. Although this tried-and-true tip is quite common, but it is also quite commonly ignored. In an ideal world, "the data speaks for itself." However, it is becoming quite clear that we need to give the data the right touch so it can say the right things to the right people. This is important because we are not just presenting the information; we are giving a call to action.

Different people are motivated by different things. So it stands to reason that if you are looking to present your data in a way that will inspire people to act on it, it will have to be framed in ways they understand. If your boss' biggest concern is saving or making money, he will probably not be inspired if you frame the data in a way that shows how it's going to make his employees' lives easier. You need to show how much the problem is costing the company and how a potential solution could save money. Framing your data this way may sway him into action. Frame your data in terms of money.

If you're from a company lucky enough to have a fat bank account, your manager might not care how much things are costing. He may only care about how much more efficient jobs become when a specific problem is addressed. Frame things in terms of time and output.

Of course, most managers have a plethora of responsibilities, so the approaches can't be entirely one-sided. Focusing on things that matter the most will always grab more attention that just stating facts that are drawn from the data. The most common things to focus on include money spent, money saved, efficiencies gained, time saved, benefits maximized, and problems minimized.

KNOW YOUR DATA

When the time comes for you to stand up in front of all your managers and present your brand-new idea, it is crucial to your success that you expect opposition. You may have spent months working on a project and have convinced yourself beyond any shadow of doubt that this is the appropriate path of action. However, the people you have to convince might have reservations due to information outside of the data that you may or may not know.

One thing that's crucial to understand is the painful truth that you may not always be right. No amount of data analysis and number crunching will turn a bad idea into a good one. Also, the reason there are people responsible for decision making is because they are trusted to have good judgement. That is why they will ask you hard questions and poke as many holes into your beautiful plans. Only after they have riddled your plans with holes, will they see whether your plan holds any merits.

I won't be able to give you a repertoire of all the objections you're going to encounter, but I will give you the best way overcome a large portion of them. **Know your data**. If your job is to make a case for or against a decision, the data is your ammunition. Failure to know your data well will cause your plan (as good as it may be) to falter once the questions start flying.

If you can't answer basic questions about the plan you're proposing, nobody will take it seriously. This is why you need to thoroughly understand the data before presenting it to others. Have aces up your sleeve. Run adjacent reports. Understand the repercussions of your suggestions. Try to forecast the probable objections your audience will bring up and answer them.

Even if giving an exact answer will require you to rerun most of the numbers and redo the entire analysis, understanding how different parameters influence the final numbers will save your presentation and reputation. Saying "Your suggestion will most likely affect the outcome in the following ways…, but I'd need some time to analyze and verify the numbers," instead of "I don't know" will prove that you understand the data well enough for your analysis to be trusted.

DOUBLE-CHECK YOUR WORK

Always double check your work. I repeat, ALWAYS DOUBLE CHECK YOUR WORK! If you are too close to your work or your experience isn't enough to validate your own numbers, find another person to run the numbers by before presenting your findings. Nothing kills your credibility faster than presenting numbers that someone in your audience can immediately shut down with facts.

It isn't easy to analyze data. Most of the time, it needs to be modified a lot before it can make sense. This is why an analyst must spend a significant amount of time ensuring that the results are sound. Presenting wrong information at best is embarrassing, but at worse it can lead to terrible decision making that can significantly set the company back.

One thing that may help is to always keep track of your emotional state while working through analysis. If you are overly stressed, rushed, distracted, or tired, you should accept that there is an increased chance of making mistakes in logic. You may miss small details, which should be a red flag to take extra care of your analysis and employ extra measures to ensure its reliability.

I understand that there will always be things outside of your control. You might have a lot going on in your personal life. You may have several tight deadlines. You may also be one of those people with their hearts on their sleeves, a stressed life, or a quick temper. Managing your emotions and stress should be a priority if you hope to turn out consistently accurate analysis. You need to keep a cool rationale and remain focused when working with data as this increases chances of producing more reliable reports.

EMPHASIZE THE IMPORTANCE AND IMPACT

I can't overstate enough the necessity to accurately portray importance and impact. When bringing up either problems or opportunities, it is easy to forego emphasizing things at the risk of being wrong. I've met many people and heard many stories where they tell their superiors about big problems coming or big opportunities only to get ignored until it's too late.

It is human nature to try to save oneself the embarrassment of being so convinced of something wrong by downplaying and avoiding assertiveness. One could also want to avoid offending their superiors or coworkers, but lack of assertiveness undermines calls to action.

"I think we may be spending a bit more money than we need to in this product line" is completely different from "We spend an extra hundred thousand dollars each month by not properly sourcing for this product line; this adds up to a potential 1.2 million dollars a year."

The first line doesn't inspire any action. The second accurately describes the impact of the problem at its current stat. It identifies the root cause and emphasizes the long-term impact of ignoring the problem. Even if it isn't a million-dollar problem, accurately portraying the problem, stating the root cause, and emphasizing the long-term impact usually leads people to reevaluate any decision that's worth all the consequences associated with it. Not only that, acting or refusing to act after they have been explicitly confronted with the weight of the decisions makes the superiors liable for the consequences of their decisions.

If it's not your job to make the decisions, you should consider it part of your job to ensure that the person making the decisions is fully aware of what their decisions mean. This is important even if it just means letting them know how much whatever decision they make will cost.

PAINT A STORY

When it comes down to presenting to others, talking about dull figures and facts (as important as they might be) might not be enough to sway people to action. You will often need to ensure that they are emotionally invested in the situation. You will need to tell a story.

Telling a story helps you to relevant facts and figures, and you chronologically present the necessary context by which to interpret these facts. Perhaps $10,000 in savings might not sway the people in your meeting. But adding the fact that that the amount is half of what is being currently spent might have a stronger influence. The $10,000 might be invested in a project that will also significantly increase revenue. It might also be available for the pool of bonuses at the end of the year.

Typical stories have three stages: the setup, the conflict, and the resolution. In most businesses, painting stories is a bit different.

The decision makers in companies are usually seasoned executives or people who understand the business well enough. This means that the set up should only highlight important factors of the background that contribute to the rest of the story.

The conflict, however, is extremely important. It needs to be framed in terms that every decision maker will understand. It needs to highlight how these problems reach across the company into the very desks of each one of the people involved in making the decision. For example, the financial comptroller might have different internal goals. If you don't portray how the current problem affects his own goals, they might not see it as a priority.

If the problem or opportunity is big enough, it might be obvious how it affects them personally. Still, assuming such things can leave some unnecessary uncertainty on the matter. If the stakeholders don't understand the weight of their decision, they might opt for indecision which could kill any momentum the resolution might have had.

The conflict is also the part of the story where you emphasize the importance and the impact of the current situation which, as I've previously mentioned, is a crucial step in calling people to action.

The resolution stage is where you bring

your professional expertise and propose a viable solution that takes into consideration everything you've previously brought up. If your solution doesn't consider all the points you previously brought up, you should also mention contingency plans or separate possible actions to address those left-over points.

This is also a good time to bring up the estimated impact of the proposed solution. The solution should be perfectly emphasized because lack of a good plan of action might lead to indecision. This will cause the problem to stall until someone else brings a viable solution to the table. The problem may even be forgotten altogether.

Painting stories with these things in mind when attempting to convince peers, bosses, or other stakeholders might provide the crucial buy-in from all the necessary parties. This allows for an easier and successful implementation of whatever plan is needed to solve the problems at hand. It may also allow the company to take advantage of any opportunities in a timely manner.

The final part of painting a story, depending on the technical capabilities and resources at hand, are visualizations. It will not be easy for everyone to grasp what you are trying to communicate based on your word alone. Visualizations can bridge that gap to visual learners, those who are hard of hearing, and distracted employees. To drive home your points, bring visualizations to the table.

Later, I'll come back to this topic after we cover visualizations.

VISUALIZATIONS

Moderate businesses and universities rely heavily on methods of visualization when there is a need to communicate information to people. From flyers to dashboards, the ability to visually portray information can go a long way towards motivating people to action. These are powerful tools to drive home important points. Their strength lies in their comparative units' strength which makes it easy for people to make sense of complex data easily.

Look at the following set of numbers

5654268.25   4934875.87
6768432.64   6946216.12   7252314.62
8595645.16   7631568.36   9064789.50
7564789.91   7821458.80   8964759.21
9645789.90   9464785.00   8921635.00
9665753.50   9946523.80   9664785.20
9945687.80

What do these numbers tell you? Honestly, not much without context. This may be sales data for the past 18 months. But the numbers wouldn't make sense to many, much less sway them into acting on them. That's if they even bothered to read them.

Let's arrange the numbers in a way we can make a bit of sense of. We'll add some context to the numbers, and present them on a line graph to show changes over time.

Now we can clearly see a positive pattern emerge. If we do some more calculations, we might also be able to add a few key take-aways so that everyone understands the impact of what we're seeing here.

Doubled sales in one year	4% average growth month-over-month	$84 million year-to-date	$156 million expected next 12 months

Now that you understand where the power behind the visualizations comes from, we can start to look at ways to optimize it.

Since most people in today's modern business world are trained in Microsoft Excel, we'll explore some of those ways. For the most part, these ways are standard across most computer software that analyzes data. With more sophisticated software, we may be able to rely on advanced or dynamic visualizations. Depending on your scope of work or the quality of results you must produce, additional skills might be necessary. But for most general analysis, the basic tools Excel provides should be enough.

CONSISTENCY PRINCIPLE

When presenting data, it is crucial to stay consistent with the information you present. A dishonest analyst deliberately deciding to be inconsistent can manipulate and misrepresent data and lead the audience to make inaccurate deductions. While you may not have deceitful intentions, it is just as easy to accidentally sway the perception of your results by not being consistent in your visualizations.

Let's say you have an upcoming presentation. You want sales numbers for two different regions.

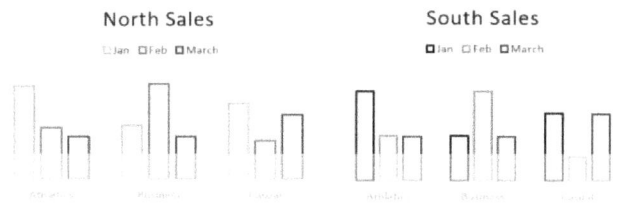

Overall the sales seem evenly distributed. One may even assume that both regions are doing similarly well. However, this could be misleading as we neglected to include labels on our presentation.

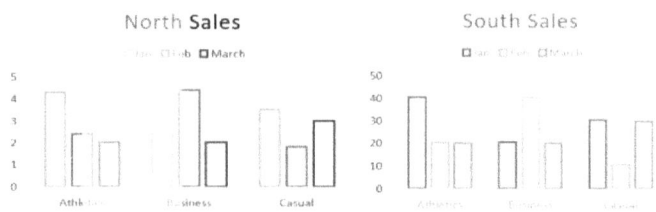

When we add labels, we can deduce that the regions have vastly different sales volumes. But it's difficult to see the difference between these two regions. Even after looking at the graphs, it might be difficult to be swayed to action based on these numbers.

Finally, once we standardize the Y-axis, we can clearly see an accurate volume comparison between the two regions. The graphs are compelling indications that management actions are needed.

By using consistent principles on our visualizations across the board, we can provide accurate information which will be used to make decisions.

TIME HORIZON

Another important consideration when it comes to portraying information accurately is the data's time horizon. When looking at things over time, it's crucial to use appropriate time horizons. Using improper time horizons can lead to making decisions with accidentally biased data.

Using the line graph provided earlier, the analysis is currently sitting at 18 months' worth of data.

This time horizon allows us to clearly see the positive trend in the data. However, if I had decided to use a 3-month time horizon instead, my results would be significantly different.

Over the past three months, the data has stayed relatively still with no clear positive or negative trend. The best we can conclude is that the sales for the next 12 months will probably stay right around the 10-million mark. There will be no significant increase or decrease, and the average month-over-month growth will be nearly zero.

If I had done a three-month analysis from March to May, I would believe there is a negative trend and my monthly sales are slowly slipping.

Data horizons are particularly important when you're showing historical data. As with most things we've talked about, there is no one-size-fits-all answer to time horizons. However, there are a few basic rules that you could use to improve your judgement.

1. Always take into consideration your current long-term and short-term goals.
2. Always try to capture the most accurate representation of the information.
3. If the industry is known to be volatile, using long time horizons will smooth out results. Short horizons could be deceiving.
4. Take into consideration your audience. Your manager might care more about his monthly performance while your CEO might care more about the company's long-term performance.
5. Keep in mind the task at hand. If you're analyzing an initiative you recently implemented, it might be necessary to only include the time of the initiative and some reference points.
6. Be aware of data swayed by unique events. A sales month might have been particularly low due to a natural disaster. It may have been high due to a sales promotion. Include extra time to accurate represent the data, and consider explaining the reasons behind these outliers

DATA AND CHARTS

Each visualization tool says something different. Some are better suited to portray certain types of information better than others. I'll briefly go over some of the most common ones to help you with your presentations.

PIE CHARTS

Pie charts are great when you are looking at percentages of a whole. With this graphic, one can clearly see the intensity of relationships of various aspects of a business and how they fit into the greater picture. This is a great way to identify priorities, points of weakness, and opportunities.

One thing though, pie charts aren't particularly good at accounting for various categories of equal values. They are, however, always a good starting point of the visualization process. They give you a few things to focus on if you ever need to prioritize your efforts.

LINE GRAPHS

Line graphs can be great at portraying information over time. They can be used to identify trends, correlations, and intensity. Line graphs can also be instrumental in monitoring business metrics such as benchmarks and key performance indicators.

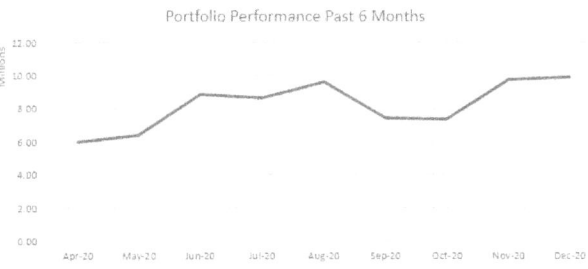

GEO MAPS

Maps can be a great way to portray relationships in a geographical context. Depending on the resources available, you can create heat maps such as the one below created in Power BI.

You could also superimpose some figures on a world map and drive your point home. Look at the map below which was created in Microsoft Excel.

BAR GRAPHS

Bar graphs can be great at comparing different categories of values. These categories include spend per supplier, sales per month, accidents per center, deliveries per day, etc. Bar graphs are the most common and are often used for a variety of purposes.

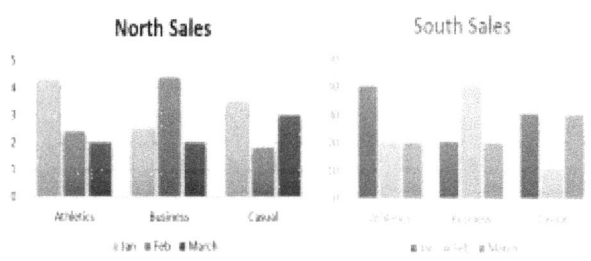

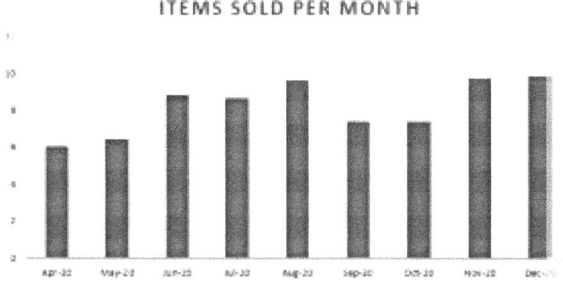

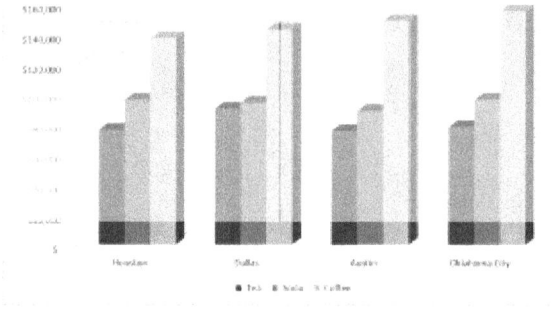

SUMMARY CARDS

There will be many situations where simple is better. There will be one number, key metric, or single point of reference being tracked that deserves the most attention. This is where summary cards come into play.

With these summary cards, you can make points that capture an important aspect of a business. It may be necessary to have a few of these to capture various points. When it comes to summary cards, it's best to prioritize and focus on the most important metrics only.

SCATTER PLOTS

This is a very powerful tool that specializes in portraying three key things between various data points: patterns, correlation, and magnitude. Oftentimes, the data isn't clear cut. Taking a step back and looking at its broad strokes instead of minute details can provide accurate representations of the data.

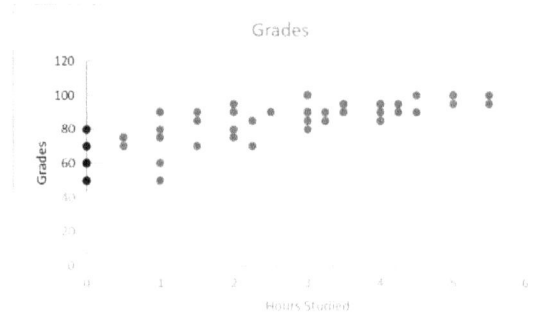

The grades above are being compared against the number of hours each of the students studied for the test. As you can see, not studying does not automatically mean you will fail. However, it will lower the probabilities that you receive a high grade on this test. It leaves an operating range between 50 and 80. Similarly, studying for over four hours does not mean the student will get a perfect score. But the range tightens, and students have a stronger probability of making high grades. The scatter chart shows a positive correlation between studying and higher grades. It also shows magnitude in that the less a student studies, the more variability there is in grades.

Let's pretend a student has a lot of responsibilities in the week of the exam. Based on this data, she estimates that if she studies for a minimum of two hours, she will have a pretty good chance of passing the test. The graph below has a trend line where we can closely estimate what the student can realistically expect with each hour of study.

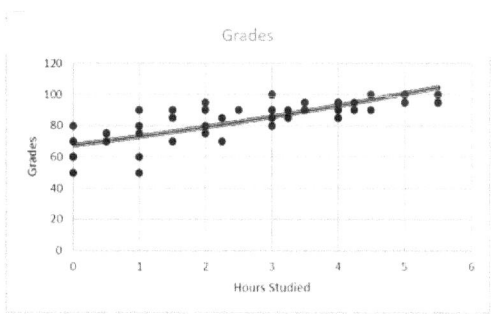

KPI

After a long journey into analytics, we will finally look at one of the main benefits of data analysis: performance management. After all the improvements have been made and ideas implemented, it is crucial for performance be monitored, controlled, and sustained. This is a lot easier said than done. The first step to performance management is deciding what needs to be measured. That alone requires foresight. With performance management, nothing is what it seems. What's more, the numbers are always only half the truth.

Let's start with the all-important "why." Deciding what to measure is the most important decision for because it will set the course and context for further decision making. If a company sets inadequate performance indicators, it could very easily implode under the weight of all other decisions henceforth. Let's take a company whose main priority is profit. This company might choose unsustainable and even unethical practices in pursuit of profit. While data analysis may point out the folly of such pursuits, the direction of the company can easily dictate the focus of the analysis thus crippling its effectiveness.

Implementing incorrect performance indicators might also have unforeseen effects on the behavior of the workforce. For example, an IT department whose main performance indicator is the count of closed tickets might lead to the careless and hasty closing of technical issues without finding root causes and fixing the problem in the first place. This effect is compounded if there are incentives or punishments for performance or lack of it.

One good place to start formulating KPIs is the organizational goals and mission. I could write another book on setting good goals, defining visions, or creating sustainable corporate missions. For the purpose of this book, we're going to skip those parts and assume the organization's mission, goals, and vision are already set in stone.

Anchoring your KPIs based on the company's greater goals is a good way to ensure that the rest of the organization does not act in a manner that contradicts the rest of the organization. This, of course, is easier said than done. Still, taking proper precautions to do this is crucial for the alignment of interests, goals, processes, and cultures.

One of the challenges with aligning KPIs

with the company's goals is that the goals are often too lofty and open to multiple interpretations. For example, a company dedicated to the greater good might act in favor of the greater good of all its stakeholders. But it will often encounter business decisions that don't prioritize these parties.

It is the responsibility of the leadership to ensure that the goals, vision, and mission are clearly understood by everyone. A lack of clarity and understanding will only cause internal misalignments and problems down the road.

Once the mindset and the direction of the KPIs are established, we must move to the next part of establishing the KPIs: understanding where the data resides and what it means. This will ensure that there are no breakdowns in the execution of the processes that produce the data which is used as a measurement of the organization's performance.

Anchoring organizational goals on values that can be easily manipulated can lead to dishonest behavior within the organization. This will make carefully selected KPIs useless because they are not objective or reliable. Also, those KPIs will make it hard for decision makers to see the information they need to make good decisions.

Anchoring organizational goals on monetary values is often the easiest and most common way to set KPIs. It's more difficult to manipulate, but it often comes with its own set of issues. The effectiveness of business decisions aimed at maximizing profits and reducing costs are among the easiest to measure. However, the risks of this strategy are plenty.

When it comes to setting a company's KPIs, it is crucial to find the appropriate balance between the axioms. This means that the organizational goals must be clearly set, difficult to manipulate, and properly measured.

Choosing KPIs that stand on those three pillars will maximize alignment in all areas of the company.

DASHBOARDS

In this last section of the book, I want to go over dashboards. We've already covered the importance of each data point. We've looked at how it's acquired, its implications, how to understand it, and how to visually present it. Now, it's time we take a step as far back as we can in order to see the grand picture.

According to Dictionary.com a dashboard is a user interface that gives a current summary, usually in graphic, easy-to-read form, of key information relating to progress and performance. This is a great definition of what a dashboard IS, but I'd like to take the definition a bit further and look at "why" and "how."

PURPOSE

Let's begin by exploring some of the reasons why dashboards might be useful. You might have purchased this book with a business need in mind, or perhaps you have just taken a role where you might need to build dashboards for upper management. Ultimately, the best case for dashboards can be summarized in two words: actionable intelligence. Whether it is you, your boss, or a set of people that are trying to understand the data. The purpose of dashboards is to provide the base for data driven decisions.

As mentioned throughout this book, data is at the core of good decision making. But oftentimes, the information is scattered across systems where it isn't easy to have all the information in one place. The problem gets compounded by the changing nature of business. Each day, companies perform trillions of transactions which generate data across the world's business systems.

The need for instant, accurate, and self-sustaining information becomes more important every day. With today's technology, it's becoming increasingly easy to set up systems to analyze the information. This is where dashboards can provide a competitive advantage, especially if they are live.

A live dashboard has one distinct advantage over standard dashboards. It updates automatically and instantly. Most dashboards are static and are updated once a day, week, or month. When they are updated depends on the urgency and business cases. For most business uses, this is enough. There is no need to spend extra resources creating a live dashboard when people only need to look at it once a week or a month. However, there will be instances when up-to-the-minute (or even second) data is crucial for decision making. In those instances, live dashboards are not only recommended but essential.

METHOD

A dashboard can simply be a collection of graphics, graphs, charts, and other visualizations that provide an overall view of a particular objective or business process. This could be done in many ways, and it's often up to the creativity of the analyst. Depending on how good one is with technology, this could be a simple as a summary page on an excel sheet, a report on a platform like Power BI or Tableau, or a website page that draws live data from the business systems.

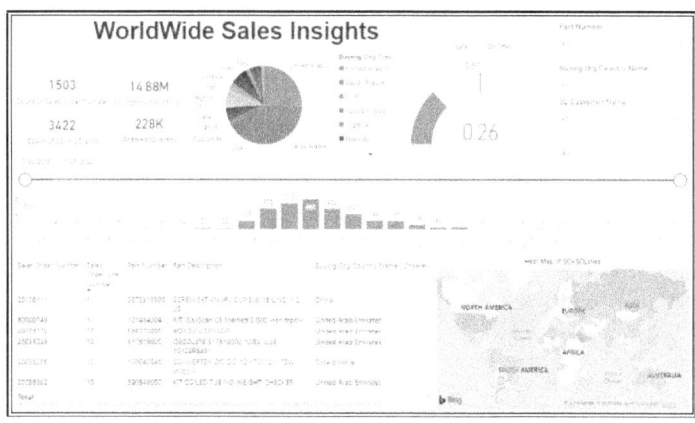

Here is a dashboard created in Power BI

for a fictional company that specializes in selling hardware around the world. It contains a lot of information on different aspects of the company and various ways to visualize the data, so I'll use it to illustrate a few of the topics below.

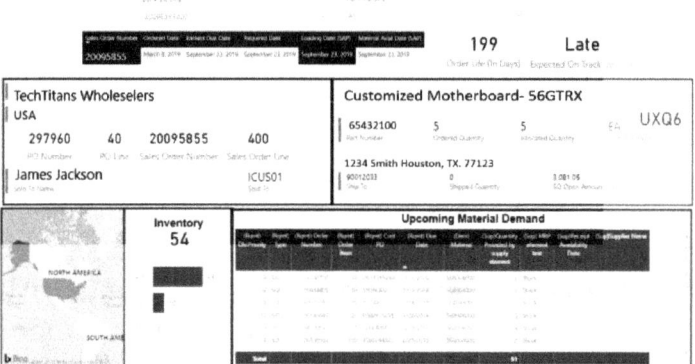

Here is a different fictional company specializing in selling trinkets and associated accessories. This one focuses on displaying information from various business systems about each specific order they get. This information includes technical details of the materials, inventory management system, and order management system.

GRAPHICS

Dashboards contain graphics which are often as simple as the company logo. These graphics can also include static or interactive pictures, backgrounds, watermarks, shapes, and lines.

These graphics could be used to organize, enhance, or provide context to the information presented on the dashboard.

The dashboards above have a few primary graphics. It has a title, some customer and PO information, and a graphic showing the country the order belongs to.

| WorldWide Sales Insights |

TechTitans Wholesalers			
USA			
297960	40	20095855	400
James Jackson			ICUS91

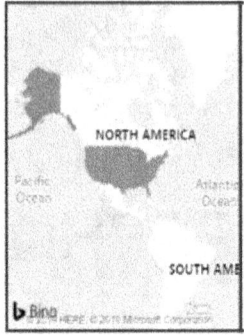

CHARTS

As mentioned in the previous chapters, charts are an important factor to understanding information. It's only natural that we include various types of charts on our dashboards. When adding charts to a dashboard, it is important not to overwhelm the audience with repetitive, difficult-to-read, or convoluted charts that need explaining to understand. As a general rule of thumb, keep your dashboards simple, concise, and readable. The point is for the audience to quickly or easily grasp the information.

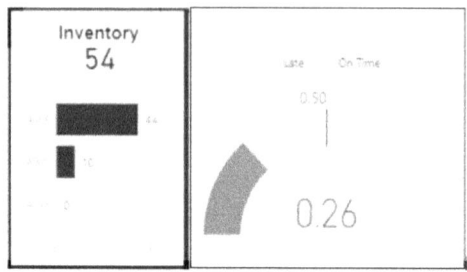
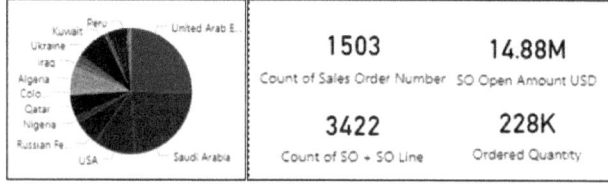

AESTHETICS

Once all the pieces of information come together, you need to focus on aesthetics before taking it to the next level. You need to make the information look good or presentable. Some people are more inclined to understand and design beauty than others. However, that is not to say there aren't a couple of principles that could be learned and replicated for the sake of professionalism and ultimately the end users.

I prefer to keep things simple, symmetrical, and uniform. However, I will admit that this design doesn't suit every situation.

TELL A STORY WITH YOUR DASHBOARD

The best advice I can give you with dashboard building is the same one I gave with reporting earlier. **Tell a story.** For dashboards (and other visual reports), there are a few concepts to keep in mind. First, people usually read from left to right and from top to bottom. So placing the starting points of information at the top or top left is usually a very good place to start. You don't want people wandering through your dashboard and looking lost. That is visually exhausting and confusing.

On the Texas trinkets dashboard, I utilized the third, top part of the screen to provide a place where users can search for what they're looking for and receive some header details once they select an order.

THE ANALYST MINDSET

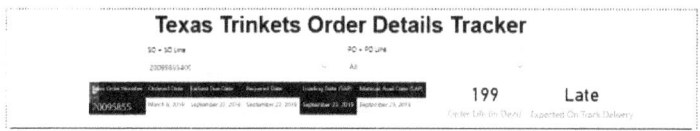

Under the title, which is the first thing they notice, a drop-down menu allows users to select the sales order or purchase order they're interested in viewing. Immediately beneath their selection, they get the important dates, a count of how long the order has been open, and whether it is late.

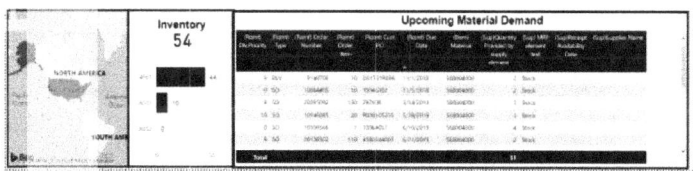

Immediately underneath, you have the buying party details and the material details. Since the information comes from different systems, the information is organized into different boxes for the user to have all the necessary information organized in a way they are used to.

Finally, on the third part of the dashboard, there are additional details that help the viewer make decisions about the order. For example, a visual of the country the order is for helps the user ascertain whether the order is going and if there are sources of supply closer. The inventory graphic shows current supply by warehouse. The last visualization shows other relevant orders that request the same material.

The story that this dashboard tells goes something like this.

First section: *"Order number(blank) placed on (blank) needs to be delivered by (blank) so it's been open for (blank) days and it's currently (either late or on time)."*

Second section: *"(Blank) company or person ordered (blank) amount of item (blank) to be delivered at (blank). (Includes necessary numbers to find more information in the original system.)*

Third section: *"For (blank country), I have a total of (blank) items available in the following locations. I also have all of these orders for the same items that I need to fill in case I need to make some changes."*

COLOR

While this version of the book is intended to be in black and white, I would be amiss to ignore the importance of colors when it comes to dashboard design.

Dashboard tools are usually well-equipped to edit colors and design. A good first step, if you're not particularly sure where to start, is to explore the different color themes available. Often, you'll find one that closely matches your company colors. If not, there are multiple online sources that can provide you with downloadable options.

Again, keep your audience in mind. People with different types of color blindness might prefer some color schemes to others. If you don't keep this in mind when you choose your color designs, they may not be impressed. There is a lot of information on the web, so consider them while making decisions on color as well.

If you're a bit more creative and have a stronger mastery of color, you might consider outside sources of inspiration. Most design experts use different color identification methods to always have the exact colors they intend, such as PMS, CMYK, RGB and HEX. If you're looking into upgrading your color abilities for dashboard creation, there are many art and design classes available.

MAINTAINING THE DASHBOARDS

Oftentimes, the issue of maintenance gets ignored when one is dealing with data analysis and dashboards.

When people build dashboards, they often focus on what they need to see right now. They forget about the data they are going to need in the future and what it's going to take to sustain it.

Sustainability is the key to good long-term data analysis and decision making. If you implement too many changes and try to analyze it using data that is inconsistent, you will be clouding your own results.

A little bit of foresight and practice can go a long way. For starters, keep in mind all that you've learned in this book as it will serve to help you make good decisions.

Standardize the information whenever possible. There is nothing worse than having to reinvent your methods each time you need a calculation because your data is coming in different forms from different sources which opens room for errors.

Use raw information when building dashboards intended to be used in the long term. Often, our data sources provide us with dirty data. However, if you need to spend hours cleaning your reports, you are not optimizing your time. Try to automate as much of the data-cleansing process as possible. This will save you a lot of time and mistakes in the future.

Automating data cleanup is one skill I recommend advancing. If you don't have advanced tools for it, you will have to get creative. Even a calculated column using an IF statement in Excel can go a long way into saving your time and making your data clean and more organized.

Often, you will have people who are not happy with your dashboards. As with any other thing in life, these people will have an opinion. Keep in mind who is asking and why they are asking. Rule of thumb, if it's your boss asking, and they're making the decisions, you should do what they ask. If it's an end user, however, be careful of implementing changes that they ask for. You could be running into a situation where you modify a dashboard to be useful to only 10% of your end users and end up ruining its usefulness to the other 90%.

Thoroughly examine requests before deciding to implement any of them. Some requests will require you to expand your scope beyond what was originally intended. Others may want you to take the information in a different direction than it needs to go. Others will try to overwhelm your dashboard with unnecessary clutter. This is where you need to master the ability to say NO!

With KPIs, be careful not to change them too often. Frequent changes may skew the intended results. Think of it as running a race. If the finish line is randomly changed during the race, some people may use this to cheat. Others may even find themselves running a race they can't possibly finish.

CLOSING REMARKS

When I started writing this book, I had one main goal in mind. I intended to help people process information in ways that ensure better decision making. In the time it took me to write The Analyst Mindset, the world continued to evolve. More and more tools became available. Technology continues its endless ever-accelerating evolution.

For this book to be useful to you in the long term, focus on the concepts rather than the technology. I tried to speak about specific technologies as little as possible in the hopes to aid this goal. But speaking about data without speaking about the technology I regularly use to dissect it is a difficult task. The technology will change. The tools will improve. The volumes of data will increase. Also, the future problems that will need to be addressed with data will continue to evolve in unimaginable ways.

After reading this book, I hope you will

continue to learn about the different tools that will help you achieve the results you are looking for.

In today's world we have seen remarkable advances in data related fields, such as the internet of things (IOT), blockchain, artificial intelligence, quantum computing, etc.

For those with more practical goals, my hope is that this book will help you advance your career. May it help you grow your business, provide for your family, and secure your place in tomorrow's data-driven world.

If The Analyst Mindset has been useful to you, pass it on to your friends and family so that it can be helpful to them as well.

Thank you for reading.

www.ingramcontent.com/pod-product-compliance
Lightning Source LLC
Chambersburg PA
CBHW071404210526
45465CB00001B/249